The Tale of Tom Kitten

The Tale of Tom Kitten

by Beatrix Potter

THE CLASSIC

Once upon a time there were
three little kittens, and their names were
Mittens, Tom Kitten, and Moppet.

They had dear little fur coats of their own;
and they tumbled about the doorstep
and played in the dust.

But one day their mother—

Mrs. Tabitha Twitchit—expected

friends to tea; so she fetched

the kittens indoors, to wash and

dress them, before the fine company arrived.

First she scrubbed their faces
(this one is Moppet).

Then she brushed their fur
(this one is Mittens).

Then she combed their tails
and whiskers (this is Tom Kitten).
Tom was very naughty,
and he scratched.

Mrs. Tabitha dressed Moppet

and Mittens in clean pinafores

and tuckers; and then she took

all sorts of elegant uncomfortable

clothes out of a chest of drawers,

in order to dress up her son Thomas.

Tom Kitten was very fat, and he
had grown; several buttons burst off.
His mother sewed them on again.

When the three kittens were ready,
Mrs. Tabitha unwisely turned them out
into the garden, to be out of the way
while she made hot buttered toast.

"Now keep your frocks clean, children!
You must walk on your hind legs.
Keep away from the dirty ash-pit,
and from Sally Henny Penny,
and from the pig-stye and the
Puddle-Ducks."

Moppet and Mittens walked down
the garden path unsteadily.
Presently they trod upon their
pinafores and fell on their noses.

When they stood up there were
several green smears!

"Let us climb up the rockery,
and sit on the garden wall,"
said Moppet.

They turned their pinafores
back to front, and went up with
a skip and a jump; Moppet's
white tucker fell down into the road.

Tom Kitten was quite unable to jump when walking upon his hind legs in trousers. He came up the rockery by degrees, breaking the ferns, and shedding buttons right and left.

He was all in pieces when he
reached the top of the wall.

Moppet and Mittens tried to
pull him together; his hat fell off,
and the rest of his buttons burst.

While they were in difficulties,

there was a pit pat paddle pat!

and the three Puddle-Ducks came along

the hard high road, marching one behind

the other and doing the goose step—

pit pat paddle pat! pit pat waddle pat!

They stopped and stood in a row,
and stared up at the kittens.
They had very small eyes
and looked surprised.

Then the two duck-birds,

Rebeccah and Jemima Puddle-Duck,

picked up the hat and tucker

and put them on.

Mittens laughed so that she fell off the wall. Moppet and Tom descended after her; the pinafores and all the rest of Tom's clothes came off on the way down.

"Come! Mr. Drake Puddle-Duck," said Moppet—"Come and help us to dress him! Come and button up Tom!"

Mr. Drake Puddle-Duck advanced in a slow sideways manner, and picked up the various articles.

But he put them on *himself*!
They fitted him even worse than
Tom Kitten.

"It's a very fine morning!"
said Mr. Drake Puddle-Duck.

And he and Jemima and Rebeccah

Puddle-Duck set off up the road,

keeping step—

pit pat, paddle pat! pit pat, waddle pat!

Then Tabitha Twitchit came down the garden and found her kittens on the wall with no clothes on.

She pulled them off the wall,

smacked them, and took them

back to the house.

"My friends will arrive in a minute,

and you are not fit to be seen;

I am affronted,"

said Mrs. Tabitha Twitchit.

She sent them upstairs; and I am
sorry to say she told her friends
that they were in bed with the
measles; which was not true.

Quite the contrary; they were not in bed;
not in the least.

Somehow there were very extraordinary noises over-head, which disturbed the dignity and repose of the tea party.

And I think that some day I shall have to make another, larger, book, to tell you more about Tom Kitten!

As for the Puddle-Ducks — they
went into a pond. The clothes all came off
directly, because there were no buttons.

And Mr. Drake Puddle-Duck,

and Jemima and Rebeccah,

have been looking for them ever since.

The Tale of Tom Kitten
by Beatrix Potter

Published by The Classic Publishing Co.
© The Classic Publishing 2013
All rights reserved. No part of publication may be reproduced,
stored in a retrieval system, or transmitted, in any form or by any means,
without the permission of the copyright holder, The Classic Publishing Co.
Color art by The Classic Publishing Co.

The Classic in Mirbookcompany Publishing Co. Ltd.
239-18, Yeonnam-dong, Mapo-gu, Seoul, Korea
Telephone : 02-3141-4421 Fax : 02-3141-4428
Web site : cafe.naver.com/mirbookcompany
E-mail : sanhonjinju@naver.com